8-09

SANITATION INVESTIGATION

Getting to Know Your Toilet

The Disgusting Story Behind Your Home's Strangest Feature

by CONNIE COLWELL MILLER

Consultant:
Rob Janus
Planterra Management Ltd.
Victoria, British Columbia

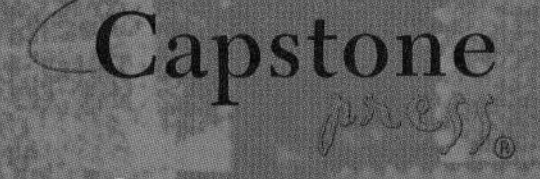

Mankato, Minnesota

Edge Books are published by Capstone Press,
151 Good Counsel Drive, P.O. Box 669, Mankato, Minnesota 56002.
www.capstonepress.com

Printed in the United States of America

Library of Congress Cataloging-in-Publication Data
Miller, Connie Colwell, 1976–
Getting to know your toilet: the disgusting story behind your home's strangest feature / by Connie Colwell Miller.
p. cm. — (Edge books. Sanitation investigation)
Summary: "Describes the history of the toilet and how people dealt with human waste prior to its invention."
Includes bibliographical references and index.
ISBN-13: 978-1-4296-1997-4 (hardcover)
ISBN-10: 1-4296-1997-X (hardcover)
1. Toilets — Juvenile literature. I. Title. II. Series.
GT476.M55 2009
392.3'6 — dc22 2008000536

Editorial Credits
Mandy Robbins, editor; Alison Thiele, designer; Wanda Winch, photo researcher; Sarah L. Schuette, photo shoot direction; Marcy Morin, scheduler

Photo Credits
The Bridgeman Art Library International/Private Collection, The Stapleton Collection/Triton Closet from a catalogue of sanitary wares produced by Morrison, Ingram & Co., Manchester, published c.1890 (colour litho), English School, (19th century), 13
Capstone Press/Karon Dubke, cover, 1, 11, 18, 20–21, 22–23, 29
Getty Images Inc./Visuals Unlimited/Dr. Dennis Kunkel, 27
The Image Works/Heritage-Images/Artmedia, 8
iStockphoto/Jeremy Clark (wood background element), cover, all; Mike Matas, 24; Sharon Dominick, 4
Photri-MicroStock, 16–17
Shutterstock/clearviewstock (yellow hazard stripes on road), 14, 26; David Huntley (push pin), 5, 7, 10, 12, 16, 21, 26; Gilmanshin (grunge background), cover, all; Herminia Lucia Lopes Serra, 15; Larisa Loftiskaya (sheet of paper with torn edges), 14, 26; Rita Jacobs, 6–7

1 2 3 4 5 6 13 12 11 10 09 08

TABLE OF CONTENTS

CHAPTERS

FEATURES

Chapter 1

YOUR OWN SUPER BOWL

Toilets help clean up a messy human function.

LEARN ABOUT:

- An important invention
- Outhouse era
- Toilet paper of a different kind

What do you have in common with movie stars, professional athletes, and the president of the United States? You all use the toilet.

The toilet just might be one of the most important inventions of all time. Toilets flush nasty waste out of our lives. The waste goes to water treatment plants, never to bother us again. Pretty slick, huh?

Life With Your Toilet

The average person uses the toilet about seven times a day. That adds up to 2,555 visits to the bathroom each year. You will spend about three years of your life just sitting — or standing — there.

EDGE FACT:

World Toilet Day is celebrated on November 19. Celebrate this year, or you'll be a party pooper!

Life With No Toilet

Just imagine your life without a toilet. You're in your bedroom getting cozy under the covers. Suddenly, you feel the urge. It's already dark outside. It's cold. The wind is blowing. Maybe it's even storming. But your body doesn't care. You have to go!

What do you do? Out you go — to the outhouse. You throw on your coat and shoes. You run out the door toward the little wooden shed. You open the creaky door. It's pitch black inside and stinks terribly, but you have to go. You have no other choice.

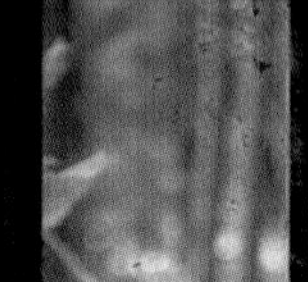

At least you lucked out with toilet paper. Someone left a magazine that you can crumple up and use.

Sound like fun? No way! Because you live in more modern times, you probably have an indoor toilet just down the hall. There might even be a warm rug on the floor. And you have soft toilet paper to wipe with and hot water for washing your hands.

You might not have thought about it before now. But admit it — life without your toilet would stink, to say the least!

People built outhouses at least 50 feet (15 meters) from their homes to keep the stink away.

EDGE FACT:

New Yorker Joseph Gayetty invented toilet paper in 1857.

Chapter 2

THE TOILET'S DIRTY HISTORY

Romans weren't concerned with privacy. They sat right next to each other while going to the bathroom.

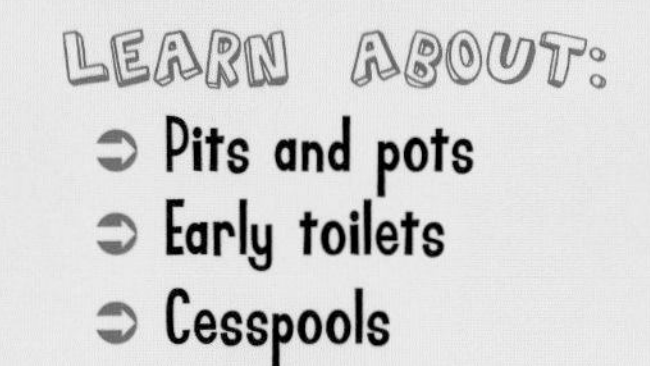

The toilet, as we know it, hasn't been around very long. Just 150 years ago, people were living up close and personal with their poop.

Pit or Pot?

Thousands of years ago, a few **civilizations** had early versions of the toilet. Some Greeks had toilets in their homes. The Romans had public restrooms. In some of these restrooms, water ran through pipes to wash away waste. In others, seats were built over water-filled ditches. Unfortunately, these early toilets disappeared along with the civilizations they came from.

civilization — an organized community

Once the ancient Greeks and Romans were gone, most people relieved themselves in a pit or a pot. Pits were holes in the ground. People dug them behind their homes and filled them up day after day. Some pits were small. People squatted, relieved themselves, and covered their waste with dirt. Larger pits were covered with wooden benches for people to sit on.

People also went in pots that they dumped outside. Sometimes they dumped out the pots in a pit. Other times they dumped them wherever it was most convenient. The pit and pot methods hung around for hundreds of years.

EDGE FACT:

In the 1100s, people in London used restrooms called garderobes. The toilets connected to pipes that emptied into a pit, moat, or river.

People in cities were more likely to use chamber pots. Crowded living conditions made it difficult for each family to have its own pit to use.

Take It Away, John!

In 1596, John Harrington came up with the idea of the flushing toilet. Harrington was the godson of England's Queen Elizabeth I. He designed the first toilet for her. Harrington's plans were similar to the toilets we have today. But almost 300 years passed before the toilet really caught on.

In 1861, an English plumber named Thomas Crapper began trying to improve Harrington's designs. By the 1880s, he sold toilets to the public out of his shop. Most of these toilets were simple bowls that swooshed away waste with a big flush of water. In most cities, this waste flowed into large dumping areas called **cesspools**.

EDGE FACT:

Between 1844 and 1855, a disease called cholera killed 20,000 people worldwide. Scientists agreed that human waste in people's food and water supply caused the disease. This knowledge helped the toilet's popularity grow.

cesspool — an underground pit that held human waste and other garbage

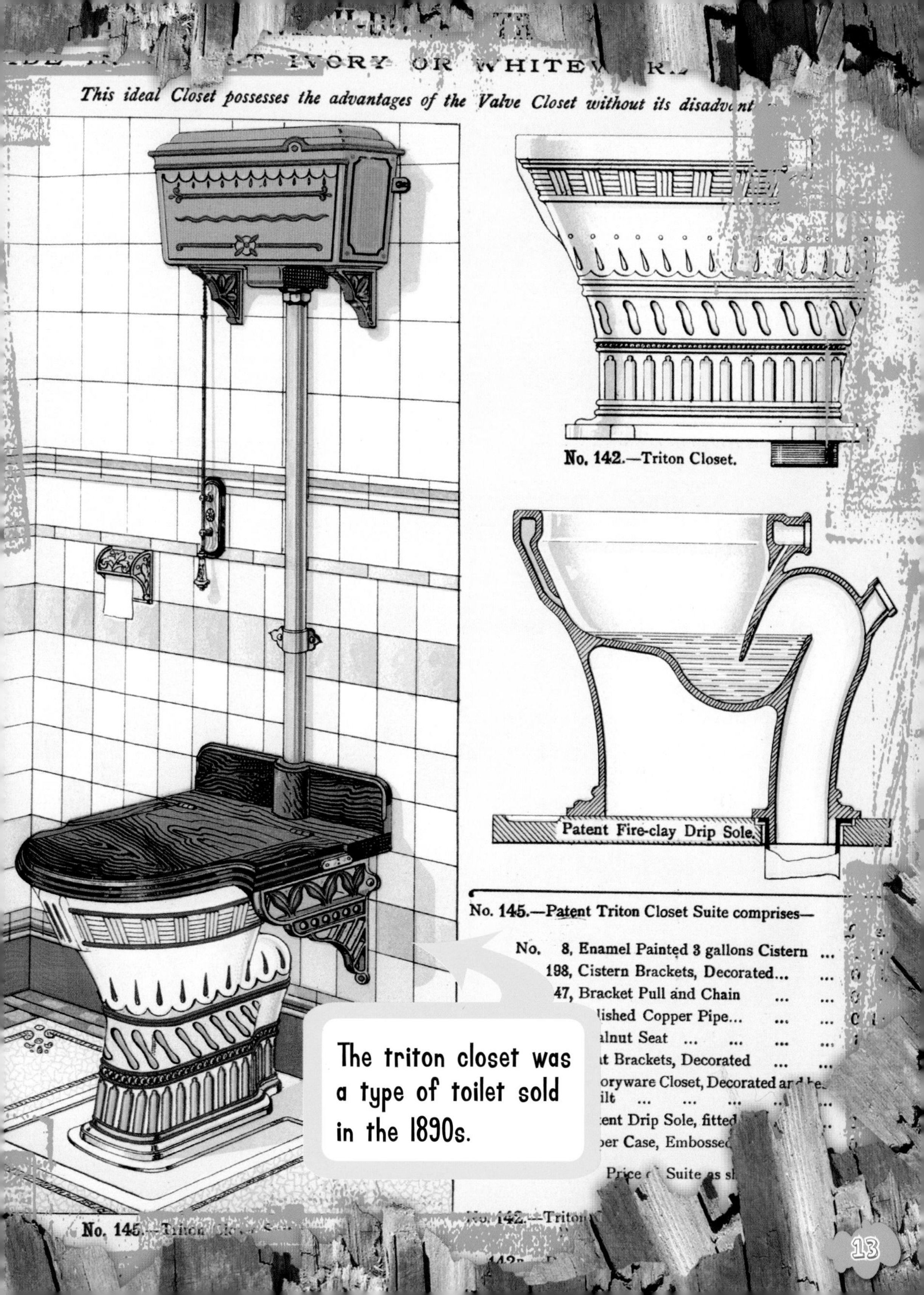

The triton closet was a type of toilet sold in the 1890s.

BUMS AWAY! THE BIDET

People in European countries often use a bidet (bih-DAY) in addition to a toilet. When they see it, Americans often think the bidet is a toilet. But it most definitely is not.

The bidet is a sinklike invention. It shoots out water in a stream to clean your bottom after you, well, dirty it. Some people in Europe use a bidet instead of toilet paper.

The bidet was invented in the 1700s in France. At that time, people bathed just once a week. But with the bidet, people could clean their underside every day. Many people still insist that the bidet is the best way to wipe.

In many European countries, the bidet sits next to the toilet.

The first toilet in the White House was installed in 1825.

At first, only wealthy people could afford toilets in their homes. The most expensive part was piping wastewater away from the home. Eventually, cities began building or improving their current sewer systems. These systems of pipes carried waste away once the toilet was flushed. Public sewer systems also made toilets cheaper to install for everyone. Soon almost every home in England and the United States had a flushing toilet.

EDGE FACT:

Toilets caught on quicker in Europe than in the United States. They became popular in the United States in the 1920s. American soldiers who served in Europe during World War I (1914 – 1918) came home impressed by the invention.

Chapter 3

FLUSHED AWAY!

Waste seems to magically disappear when you flush it down the toilet.

LEARN ABOUT:

- Sewage suction
- Very important valves
- Ready for round two

You're watching your favorite TV program when nature calls. You head to the bathroom and do your business. After you flush and wash your hands, you're done. But have you ever wondered what your toilet is doing while you head back to the couch?

Sucked Clean

The most important part of the toilet is a pipe called the **siphon**. Without it, your poop would never leave your bathroom. Look into your toilet bowl. The hole in the bottom is the top opening of the siphon.

The siphon works like a straw. It sucks the water and waste in your toilet down into the sewer. Aren't you glad you're not on the sucking end of that straw?

siphon — a bent tube through which liquid is sucked upward and then back down

On most toilets, a chain connects the handle to the flush valve.

flush valve

The Flush

On many toilets, the handle is connected to a chain on the inside of the tank. When you flush, the chain pulls up the **flush valve** inside the tank.

The flush valve keeps about 2 gallons (7.6 liters) of water in the tank. The water is ready, waiting to wash away your waste. When you flush, the valve releases the water, and it floods the toilet bowl. All that water really gets the siphon going. The siphon sucks the tank water, and whatever you put into it, right down.

EDGE FACT:

The National Energy Policy Act of 1995 requires new toilets to use 1.6 gallons (6 liters) of water or less per flush. But many homes have older units that use up to 6 gallons (23 liters)!

flush valve — a movable part that controls the flow of water in a toilet

Fill It Up!

Many toilet tanks have a plastic ball called a float. It floats in the tank water. When you flush, the water empties out, and the float falls to the bottom. This triggers the **refill mechanism** to open a valve that lets water pour back into the tank. The flush valve goes down, and the tank fills up with water again.

After the float reaches the top of the tank, the tank is full. Your toilet is now ready to flush again. This entire process takes less than a minute. You can tell when the tank is full because your toilet stops making noise.

refill mechanism — a floatation device and a valve that work together to refill the tank water in a toilet

Chapter 4
THE FILTHY FACTS

Because outhouse toilets don't flush, all of the germs from waste just sit there.

LEARN ABOUT:

- Your toilet's dirty secrets
- Life before toilet paper
- Germs and your toothbrush

Your toilet is one of the most amazing features in your home. But it also has the dirtiest job in the house.

What Goes In?

Your bodily waste goes into your toilet, right? But think for a minute. How many people live in your home? How many toilets do you have?

The average person poops once a day and releases 2 pints (.9 liters) of urine a day. Multiply that by how many people live in your home. Now you're getting a picture of just how much waste gets dumped into your toilet.

Wipe Out!

Waste isn't the only thing that spends a lot of time in your toilet. Toilet paper does, too. But toilet paper, like your toilet, is a fairly new invention.

Before toilet paper, people wiped with all sorts of things. They used newspaper, wool, straw, hay, grass, moss, and corncobs. The ancient Romans used a long stick with a sponge on the end. They kept the spongy end in a bucket of salt water between uses. Everyone in the house or the public restroom used the same gross stick. Some people in Europe and Asia even used their left hands! This is why shaking hands is traditionally done with the right hand.

Modern toilet paper was invented in 1857. It didn't become popular until the 1880s. And until 1935, it still occasionally contained wooden splinters. Ouch!

Edge Fact:

The average person uses 57 sheets of toilet paper per day.

Bacteria are too tiny to see without a microscope. But they can make you very sick.

Human waste is made up of a combination of things. There's a lot of water and bits of undigested food. Eight percent of all solid waste is **bacteria**. Your body shoves out these tiny germs to keep you healthy. And where do the germs end up? Clinging to the toilet bowl.

bacteria – microscopic living things that can cause disease

What Comes Out?

The toilet's job is to get rid of gross stuff. But your toilet isn't perfect. Some gross things hang around.

Flushing creates a powerful force of water. When you flush, invisible bits of waste shoot out of the toilet. If your toothbrush is nearby, it will get doused in germs. You should keep your toothbrush in a cupboard or a drawer. Always close the toilet lid before you flush. This can keep germy bits from flying everywhere.

Bacteria also get on your hands when you wipe. Wash your hands, or these germs could end up all over your house. You wouldn't want bacteria from the bathroom to end up on your dinner fork!

Out the End

Now you know the truth about "the throne," the gist of "the john," the scoop on poop. Where would we be without the toilet? We'd all be squatting over a pit or a pot, and the world would be a much filthier place!

If bacteria from the toilet get on your toothbrush, where do you think they will go next? That's right – your mouth!

Glossary

bacteria (bak-TEER-ee-uh) — microscopic living things; some bacteria cause disease.

bidet (bih-DAY) — a low, sinklike bathroom fixture with a faucet that points up; a bidet is used to wash a person's bottom area.

cesspool (SESS-pool) — a pit in the ground that holds human waste and other garbage

civilization (si-vuh-ly-ZAY-shuhn) — an organized and advanced society

float (FLOTE) — an object that floats in the toilet tank and regulates the water level

flush valve (FLUSH VALV) — a movable part in a toilet tank that controls the flow of water in a toilet

refill mechanism (REE-fil MEK-uh-niz-uhm) — a floatation device and a valve that work together to refill the tank water in a toilet

siphon (SYE-fuhn) — a bent tube through which liquid can drain upward and then back down

Read More

Harper, Charise Mericle. *Flush!: The Scoop on Poop Throughout the Ages.* New York: Little, Brown, 2007.

Krensky, Stephen. *What's the Big Idea?: Four Centuries of Innovation in Boston.* Watertown, Mass.: Charlesbridge, 2008.

Lunis, Natalie. *Household Inventions: From Toilets to Toasters.* Which Came First? New York: Bearport, 2006.

Internet Sites

FactHound offers a safe, fun way to find Internet sites related to this book. All of the sites on FactHound have been researched by our staff.

Here's how:

1. Visit *www.facthound.com*
2. Choose your grade level.
3. Type in this book ID **142961997X** for age-appropriate sites. You may also browse subjects by clicking on letters, or by clicking on pictures and words.
4. Click on the **Fetch It** button.

FactHound will fetch the best sites for you!

INDEX